Letter to a Friend

by Lola M. Schaefer

Table of Contents

How Did I Write and Mail My Letter?

Today I wrote a letter to my friend Derek who lives far, far away.

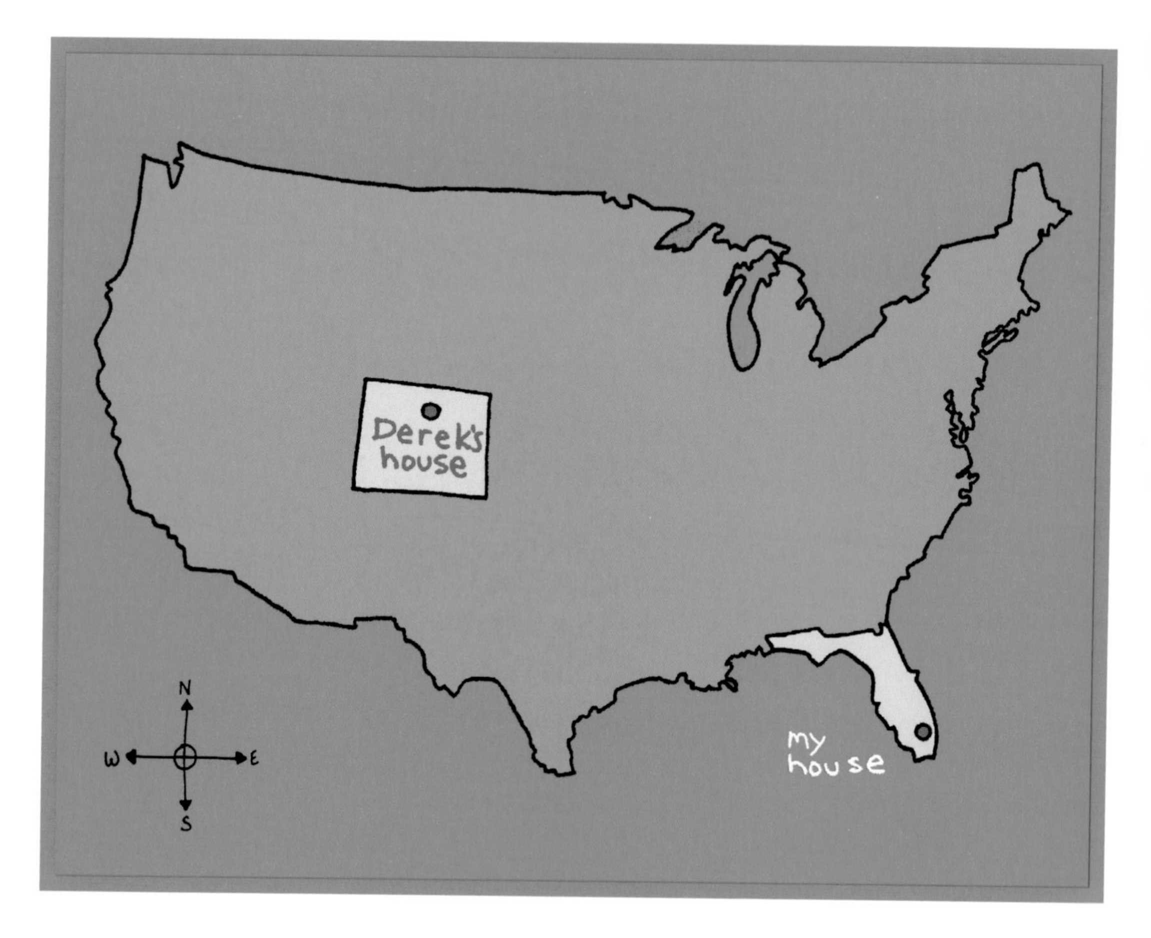

December 10

Dear Derek,

How are you?
I can't wait to see you.
Pack your shorts and
t-shirts. It is sunny
and warm here.

Your friend,
Matt

I wrote Derek's name and address
on an envelope.

I put a **stamp**
on the top right corner.

I wrote my address
in the top left corner.

my address

Matt Holloway
400 Sunshine Way
Miami, Florida 33101

Derek Jones
100 Main Street
Denver, Colorado 80201

my friend's address

What Happened to My Letter at the Post Office?

I went to the **post office** and mailed my letter. The **clerk** said it would take only a few days for my letter to get to Derek.

Then my letter was **postmarked**.
It was put into a tray with other letters that were going to the same place.

A postmark shows the date a letter was mailed and from where it was mailed.

How Did My Letter Get from My Town to My Friend's House?

Later that day, **mail handlers** put all the mail into **mail trucks**. Some trucks took mail to other post offices nearby. My letter did not go on these trucks.

My letter went in a truck that took mail to the airport. Workers took my letter and all the other mail from the truck and put it on an airplane.

Airlines carry mail all over the country for the post office.

My letter flew miles and miles across the country.

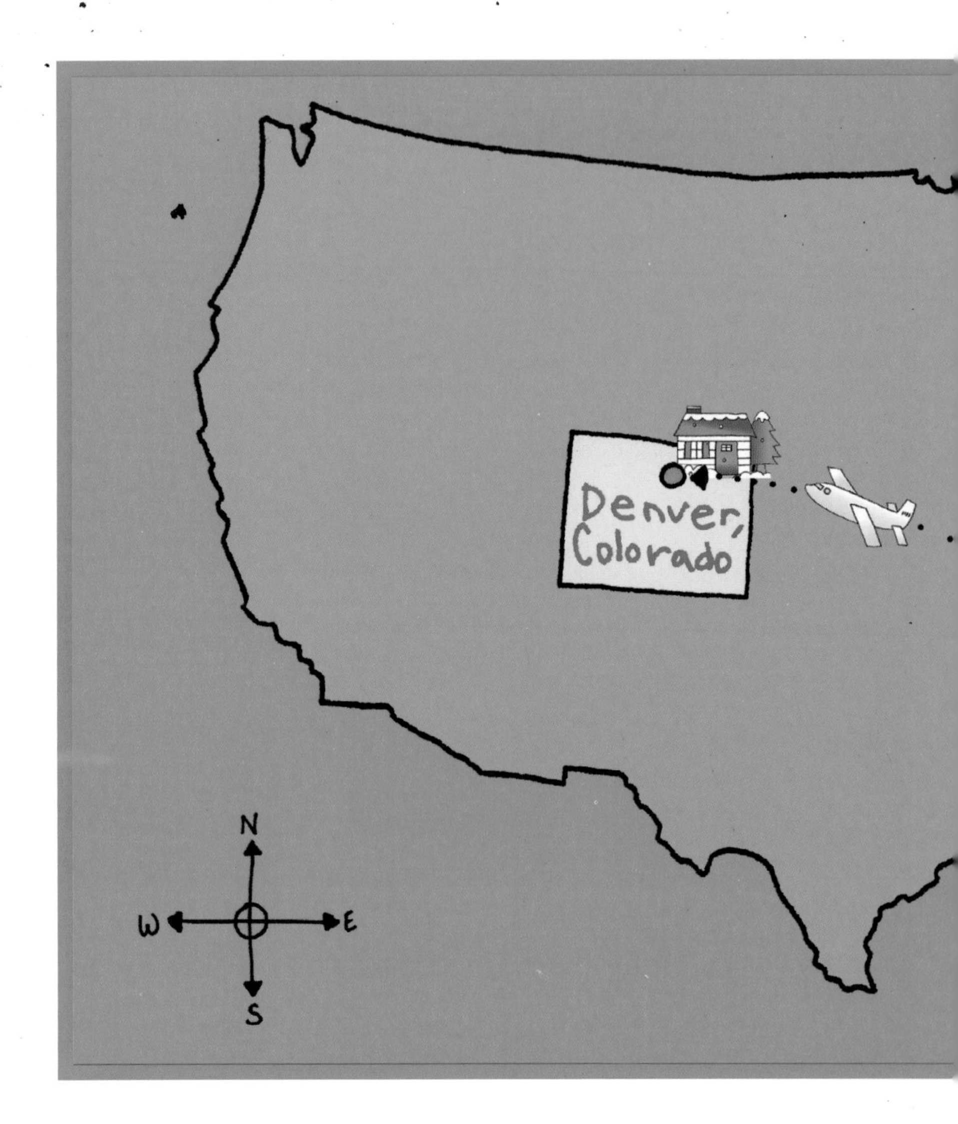

Later that day, the airplane landed at an airport near Derek's house.

Then mail handlers took the mail from the plane and put it onto trucks.

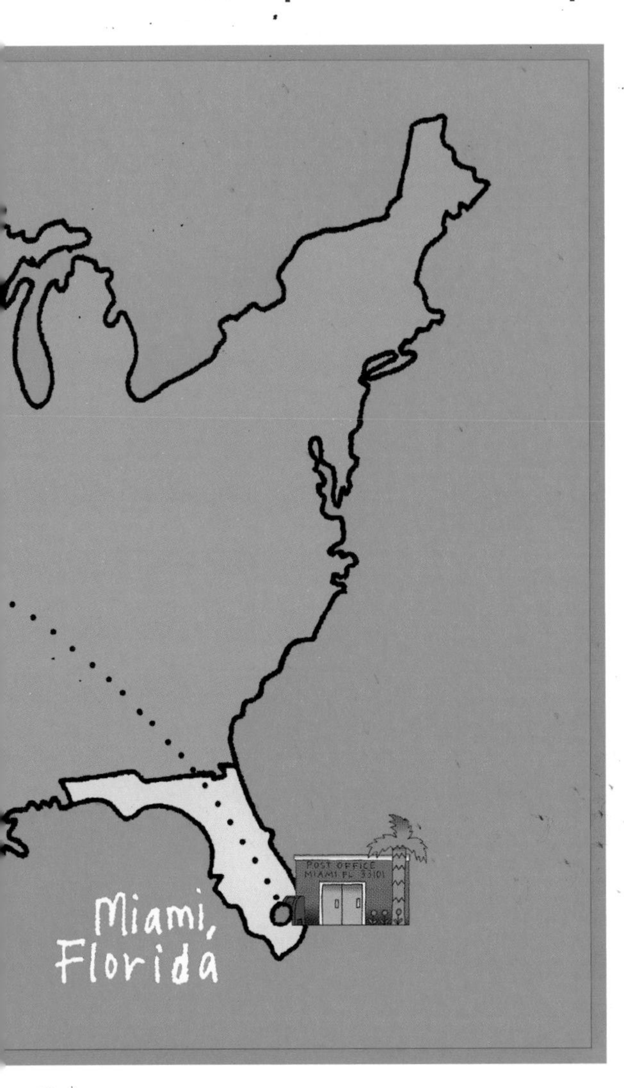

These mail trucks took my letter
and all the other mail
to the post office in Derek's city.

The next day, the clerks sorted the mail to go to the different parts of the city. Then a **mail carrier** brought my letter to Derek's house.

Derek found the letter in his **mailbox** and read it right away.

Derek wrote a letter back to me. It was in my mailbox a few days later.

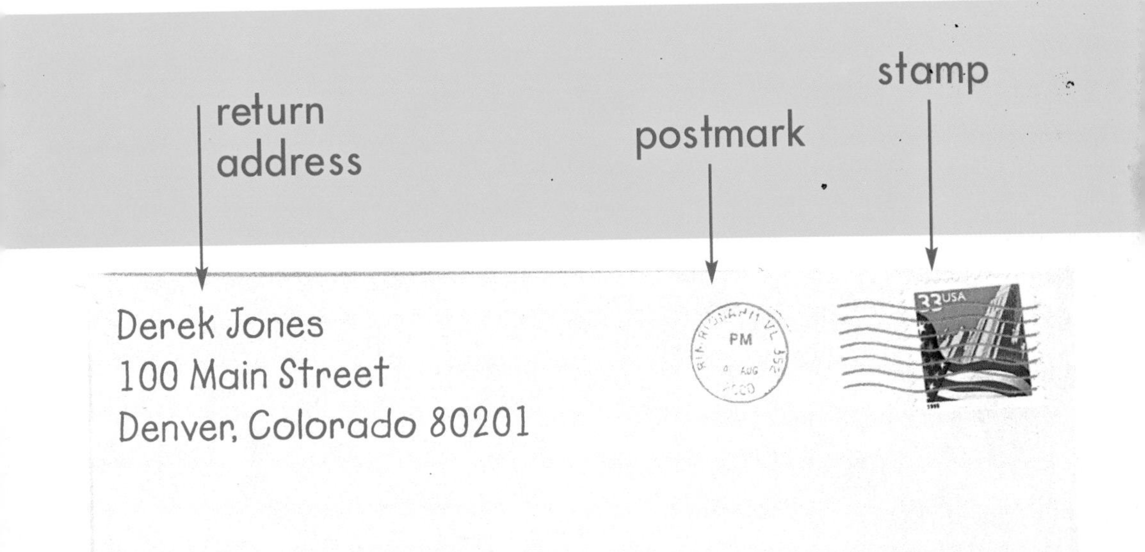

The **return address** is the address from which the letter is being sent. The **mailing address** is where the letter is going.

December 13

Dear Matt,

I just got your letter today. I am coming to see you in four days. I don't know if I can wait that long! Can we go to the zoo? Can we swim in the ocean? We will have lots of fun! See you soon.

Your friend,
Derek

I read Derek's letter and looked at the postmark. He said he would be coming in four days. And he did!

How Did Matt's Letter Travel?

1. Matt took his letter to the post office.

2. The envelope was postmarked.

3. The letter was put into a tray with other letters.

4. The mail was put onto an airplane.

5. The airplane flew to Derek's city.

6. The mail truck took the letter to the post office.

7. The mail clerk sorted the mail.

8. The mail carrier took the letter to Derek's house.

Glossary

clerk (CLERK): A person who works in an office

mail carrier (MAYL KAIR-ee-er): A person who delivers mail

mail handlers (MAYL HAND-lerz): People who sort the mail in the post office

mail trucks (MAYL TRUKS): Trucks that carry mail to different places

mailbox (MAIL-bahks): A place near a home that holds the mail that is received

mailing address (MAYL-ing a-DRESS): The address of the person to whom a letter is being sent

post office (POHST OFF-iss): The place in a community that handles the mail and sells stamps

postmarked (POST-markt): Marked to show when and where a letter was mailed

return address (RIH-tern a-DRESS): The address of the person sending a letter, placed on the top, left corner of the envelope

stamp (STAMP): A small label that is glued to a letter to show payment for delivery

Index